The Upside-Down, Inside-Out, Backwards, Oopsy-Daisy Book

The Upside-Down, Inside-Out, Backwards, Oopsy-Daisy Book

Mary Hollingsworth

Illustrated by Daniel J. Hochstatter

& Dennis Edwards

Concordia Publishing House

God made everything just right,
Like nighttime dark and daytime light.
But what if everything turned 'round,
And right-side-up was upside-down?

If right-side-in turned wrong-side-out,
And forward took a backward route,
What kind of world would we find then?
Well, turn the page, and let's begin.

The sky's not blue but creamy yellow, And Mr. Sun's a square-blue fellow.

Since clouds are brown, they don't hold water;
But dirt and mud rain down together.

The grass is orange, and goats are red,
And trees grow down, not up, instead.

White is black, and black is white.
We work at night and sleep in light.

Pigs have beaks, and birds have snouts.
Outs are ins, and ins are outs.

Rainbows smile instead of frown;
And gravity pulls up, not down.

People walk on hands, not feet;
And candy's sour,
but medicine's sweet.

Pink flamingos turn lime green.
Redbirds change to purple sheen.

Horses fly while eagles walk,
And kangaroos have learned to talk.

Dogs meow, and
kittens bark,
And nothing's nicer
than a shark.

Zebras' stripes go rainbow wild.
Baboons are tame, but folks are wild;

So people live
inside the zoo,
And monkeys point
and stare at you.

Cows give root
beer in big pails.

Fish have fur, and
ducks have scales.

People's skin is aqua blue.
(I don't know
what to think,
do you?)

And then whatever would we do
If you were me, and I were you?

It seems to me that we can be
Quite content with what we see—
Where skies are blue, and grass is green,
And raindrops wash the world so clean.

God knows everything—He does!
He knows just what to do for us,
Like sending Jesus, His own Son,
To share His love with everyone.

I'm not at all surprised, are you,
That God knew just what He should do?
He made our world exactly right—
Just look at this amazing sight!